AUSTRALIA'S SCARIEST CREATURES

BY JOHN LESLEY

DEADLY SNAKES

REDBACK publishing

First published 2024 by
Redback Publishing
PO Box 357 Frenchs Forest NSW 2086
Australia

www.redbackpublishing.com
orders@redbackpublishing.com

ISBN 978-1-761400-41-4

Author: John Lesley
Editor: Caroline Thomas
Designer: Redback Publishing
Original illustrations © Redback Publishing 2024
Originated by Redback Publishing

Acknowledgements
Abbreviations: l—left, r—right, b—bottom, t—top, c—centre, m—middle
We would like to thank the following for permission to reproduce photographs: Shutterstock; p18tl IG: divecycle, CC BY-SA 4.0 <https://creativecommons.org/licenses/by-sa/4.0>, via Wikimedia Commons; p22tl Paul Harrison, CC BY-SA 4.0 <https://creativecommons.org/licenses/by-sa/4.0>, via Wikimedia Commons; p22br Happytrails86, CC BY-SA 4.0 <https://creativecommons.org/licenses/by-sa/4.0>, via Wikimedia Commons; p25cl Michael Allen Smith from Seattle, USA, CC BY-SA 2.0 <https://creativecommons.org/licenses/by-sa/2.0>, via Wikimedia Commons

NATIONAL LIBRARY OF AUSTRALIA
A catalogue record for this book is available from the National Library of Australia

CONTENTS

Eastern Brown Snake 4
Tiger Snake 6
Taipan 8
Red-bellied Black Snake 10
Mulga Snake 12
Copperhead 14
Death Adder 16
Sea Snakes 18
Diamond Python 20
More Australian Snakes 22
World's Most Venomous Snakes 24
Snake Basic Facts 26
Snake Adaptations 28
Snakes as Pets 30
Glossary (Snake Word List) 31
Index 32

EASTERN BROWN SNAKE

Pseudonaja textilis

Australia's deadliest snake is the eastern brown snake. Up to two metres long, thin and plain brown, the snake is very dangerous. It will bite and inject venom that can kill a person.

LIFECYCLE

After mating in the spring, the female lays about ten to twenty eggs a few weeks later. Young snakes look after themselves as soon as they hatch. You might sometimes see them wriggling through long grass in a garden, looking at first glance like big worms.

HABITAT

Eastern brown snakes live in the eastern regions of Australia in many types of habitats, from bush and scrub to grasslands, and even in suburban gardens. In the bush, they shelter in rock crevices and may take over unused rabbit burrows. Near gardens or farms, they will hide in sheds and under piles of rubbish. They prefer the cool, damp and semi-arid parts of Australia, and they do not live in alpine regions or deserts.

FACT

The eastern brown snake bites more people than any other snake in Australia!

FACT FILE

Length: up to 2 metres
Colour: plain brown in a variety of shades
Venomous: yes
Habitat: bush, farms, gardens in eastern Australia
Life span: about 10 years
Scientific name: *Pseudonaja textilis*
People bitten and hospitalised each year: about 200

FACT

About 200 people each year go to hospital after being bitten by this snake!

FOOD

Eastern brown snakes eat rodents, frogs, lizards, eggs and birds. They will even eat each other if they get the chance. They hunt their prey and inject it with venom to stop it from struggling so they can then swallow it.

CONSERVATION

Eastern brown snakes are not under threat of extinction. They even increase in numbers when there is an abundance of food, such as rats and mice, after a good crop-growing season. Predators include feral dogs and cats, and birds of prey such as owls, hawks and eagles. Humans kill the snakes out of fear, or run over them accidentally with cars.

VENOM AND BITING

Although the eastern brown snake has tiny fangs, the venom it injects can be deadly to humans. A bite can result in paralysis and unstoppable bleeding. A person may not realise they have been bitten until they start to feel sick.

TIGER SNAKE

Notechis scutatus

The tiger snake has a reputation in Australia as a dangerous and aggressive creature that can kill you.

LIFECYCLE

Mating takes place in the summer. Male tiger snakes fight with each other, and the winner mates with the female. Tiger snakes are unusual in that they do not lay eggs. Instead, up to twenty baby snakes are born at a time, ready to hunt and catch their own food almost right away. Not laying eggs is an adaptation that means there are no defenceless eggs that could be a meal for predators.

HABITAT

Tiger snakes live in bushland, grassland and in wetlands. They inhabit most of southern Australia, where they like to be near fresh water. Their two habitats on the western and eastern coastal regions are separated by the dry Nullarbor Plain. They can climb into trees and also get into the roofs of buildings. In the bush, they live in hollow logs, disused animal burrows and under rocks and forest litter.

FACT

The deadly tiger snake can climb trees and get into roof spaces!

FACT

If you go swimming in a creek, you could find a tiger snake under the water!

FACT FILE

Length: 1-2 metres
Colour: grey and cream stripes, or all black
Venomous: yes
Habitat: Southern Australia and Tasmania
Life span: about 10 years
Scientific name: *Notechis scutatus*
People bitten and hospitalised each year: about 60

FOOD

Tiger snakes eat small animals such as frogs, birds, lizards and rodents. They hunt their food and paralyse it with venom so it will stop moving. They will venture under water for short periods when hunting for frogs.

CONSERVATION

Tiger snake populations are mostly stable across their habitats. Their main predators are birds of prey, including kookaburras. Humans are so scared of them that tiger snakes are usually killed on sight. They are also accidentally killed on roads.

VENOM AND BITING

Tiger snakes are very aggressive and will not back down if they feel threatened. Instead, they raise their head and flatten it in a similar way to a cobra. Their venom can kill a human. They hiss in anger and, when they strike, they embed their half-centimetre-long fangs deep into the wound.

TAIPAN

Oxyuranus

There are two types of taipan in Australia. They both have extremely potent venom, but the inland taipan is the deadliest. Its venom may be the most toxic of any snake in the world.

COASTAL TAIPAN

The coastal taipan has a brown body and pale head. The belly is lighter coloured and may have orange patches.

LIFECYCLE

After mating, the female lays about ten eggs in a hidden spot. The juvenile snakes are over forty centimetres long when they hatch out a few months later.

HABITAT

This snake lives in the tropical regions of eastern Queensland and northern Australia. It likes wetter surroundings than its inland relative and is found in forests, bush and farmland. Near towns, it will hide under piles of rubbish.

FOOD

Coastal taipans eat small animals such as rats, mice and native mammals. They use their excellent eyesight when hunting and can pick up a scent using their tongue.

VENOM AND BITING

Before biting, the taipan stops moving. It then bites several times, with quick bursts, each of which injects more venom through large fangs. They wait for the venom to take effect before trying to swallow their prey.

FACT

COASTAL TAIPAN

Taipans bite multiple times – they don't give up!

FACT

Inland taipan venom may be the most toxic of any snake in the world!

FACT FILE

Length: 2 metres
Venomous: yes
Habitat: Queensland, northern Australia, New South Wales and South Australia
Life span: about 10 years
Scientific name:
Oxyuranus scutellatus (coastal taipan)
Oxyuranus microlepidotus (inland taipan)
People bitten and hospitalised each year: about 5

FACT

People frequently confuse the coastal taipan with the eastern brown snake.

INLAND TAIPAN

The inland taipan lives in semi-arid areas of Queensland, New South Wales and South Australia. It has a brown back and a yellow belly. It is rarely seen by people and its conservation status is not certain. They eat rodents, small mammals and birds.

FIERCE SNAKE

The inland taipan is less aggressive than the coastal taipan, and very few attacks on humans are recorded. If someone does get too close, this snake will strike numerous times and inject venom. It's not surprising that its common name is the 'fierce snake'.

RED-BELLIED BLACK SNAKE

Pseudechis porphyriacus

FACT

This snake will come inside if you leave a door open!

The red-bellied black snake is a large, impressive snake that is often found in the outer suburbs of Sydney, where it seeks shade, food and water in gardens. They are inquisitive snakes, and will move slowly around a lawn, looking for food. They will even climb steps and enter a house if a door is left open, or just peer through the glass to see what is inside.

A red-bellied black snake can strike forward for at least half its own body length. A dog that is annoying it will have to be quick to leap backwards before being bitten.

HABITAT

Red-bellied black snakes live in dense bush and in open fields and forests along the middle parts of the eastern coastal regions of Australia. In paddocks, they like to lie in the sun. They enjoy being near water, so are often found basking on rocks beside a stream or creek in the bush. Bushwalkers often make a lot of noise, so the red-bellied black snake will usually have hidden itself long before they can get close.

FACT FILE

Length: 2 metres
Colour: glossy black with a red or creamy-pink belly
Venomous: yes
Life span: about 20 years
Scientific name: *Pseudechis porphyriacus*
People bitten and hospitalised each year: about 80

LIFECYCLE

This snake does not lay eggs. A few months after mating in the spring, the female gives birth to about ten live snakes that are around thirty centimetres long.

FOOD

Red-bellied black snakes eat a variety of animals, including small mammals, frogs and lizards. They will even hunt in water for a meal of fish.

CONSERVATION

Juveniles are eaten by birds of prey, but cats and dogs are usually the only animals prepared to tackle a fully-grown red-bellied black snake. Since these snakes are dependent on clean water in bushland, they are susceptible to being severely affected by the destruction of this type of habitat for human use.

VENOM AND BITING

Because of its outstanding colouring, many people think the red-bellied black snake must be extremely venomous. Actually, its venom is a little less toxic than many other types of snakes, but it will still cause severe illness if a bite is not treated, particularly in children.

FACT

The first scientist to describe this snake, in 1794, didn't think it was venomous!

MULGA SNAKE

Pseudechis australis

The mulga snake is one of the heaviest snakes in Australia, apart from the pythons.

LIFECYCLE

The female lays about ten eggs a few weeks after mating. The eggs hatch after two or three months.

HABITAT

There are very few places in Australia where you would not meet a mulga snake. They live in dense forests, grassland and deserts, although not in the far south of the country.

FOOD

Mulga snakes eat birds and eggs, small mammals, frogs and lizards.

VENOM AND BITING

The mulga snake produces a large amount of venom. When they get angry, they will hiss and writhe before striking, leaving a large and painful wound.

FACT

They don't let go after biting and keep on injecting more venom!

FACT FILE

Length: over 2 metres

Colour: shiny copper brown back with a paler belly

Venomous: yes

Habitat: all of Australia except for the most southern regions

Scientific name: *Pseudechis australis*

People bitten and hospitalised each year: rare

FACT

Mulga snakes live across more parts of Australia than any other snake.

COPPERHEAD

Austrelaps

Austrelaps ramsayi

FACT

Some copperheads live where snow falls!

Copperheads have brown scales with a copper-coloured sheen on their back. There are three different species in Australia.

LIFECYCLE

Copperheads give birth to live juvenile snakes and they do not lay eggs.

HABITAT

The copperhead prefers cool, temperate areas and is not found in arid or desert regions. Because of this, they are most numerous in the southeast of Australia. They like to be near water and are surprising because some live at altitudes where snow falls. This is a rarity for any snake since they are all cold-blooded and need warm surroundings to raise their body temperatures in order to be active.

Austrelaps labiali

FOOD

Copperheads prefer to eat other reptiles, as well as birds, eggs, frogs and insects.

FACT FILE

Length: about 50 centimetres
Colour: shiny copper brown
Venomous: yes
Scientific names:
Austrelaps labialis
Austrelaps superbus
Austrelaps ramsayi
People bitten and hospitalised each year: rare

FACT

They are happy to eat their own babies!

CONSERVATION

The smaller types of copperhead snake are under threat of extinction.

VENOM AND BITING

Copperheads are not usually aggressive and will prefer to slither away rather than stay and fight. However, if cornered, they will flatten themselves, hiss and thrash from side to side in an attempt to look scarier. Their bite will cause sickness and needs immediate attention.

DEATH ADDER

Acanthophis antarcticus

With such a fearsome name, you would be forgiven for thinking that the death adder must be the most dangerous snake in Australia. While its venom is very toxic, it is not the most venomous snake that Australia has.

The death adder has a short, solid body, with a wide head. It does not search and hunt for its prey, but prefers to lie hidden under leaves or stones and then strike when a suitable meal passes by. It has a tiny, thin tail end which it wiggles to attract prey, who think it is a worm or insect they might want to eat. This habit of hiding just under the surface litter leads to people treading on them and being bitten as a result.

LIFECYCLE

Death adders do not lay eggs but give birth to about twenty live juveniles.

HABITAT

Death adders do not live in the very coldest or hottest parts of Australia, but are found throughout a variety of other habitats across the country.

FACT

Their fangs can grow to nearly a centimetre long! OUCH!

FACT

A death adder shakes the tip of its tail to lure victims to it.

FACT FILE

Length: about 1 metre
Colour: bands of brown and grey
Venomous: yes
Scientific name: *Acanthophis antarcticus*
People bitten and hospitalised each year: about 10

FOOD

They eat reptiles, birds, frogs and mammals.

VENOM AND BITING

Death adders have large fangs to deliver their venom. Because they have short bodies, they usually bite the lower legs and feet of an unsuspecting person who steps on them.

SEA SNAKES

TURTLE-HEADED SEA SNAKE

About thirty or more types of sea snake can be found in the seas and oceans around the Australian coast. Sea snakes have evolved to live in the water, but they still need to come to the surface to breathe air. They can close off their noses when in the water.

Their flattened tails are perfect for swimming. They hunt for their food in the water and not on land. Some sea snakes look like eels, but you can tell that you have seen a snake if it does not have a fin along its back. Only eels have a dorsal fin. Sea snakes have venom but rarely attack people in the water.

Most sea snakes give birth to live young, to avoid the problems of laying eggs in water and of keeping predators away from the vulnerable eggs. The juveniles are able to swim away and look after themselves straight after birth.

FACT

Most sea snakes have extremely strong venom!

FACT

Sea snakes have adapted to live in the ocean and cannot survive for long on land.

OLIVE SEA SNAKE

This snake has a grey-green body and is found in waters along the east coast of Australia.

YELLOW-BELLIED SEA SNAKE

This snake has a bright yellow belly, black back and a spotted, flattened tail.

ELEGANT SEA SNAKE

A very long, thin snake with dark and light grey stripes.

REEF SHALLOWS SEA SNAKE (DUBOIS' SEA SNAKE)

One of the most venomous snakes in the world.

TURTLE-HEADED SEA SNAKE

This snake has black and yellow bands and a flattened tail.

DIAMOND PYTHON

Morelia spilota spilota

As the name suggests, diamond pythons have triangular patterns all along their bodies. They have a blunt nose, heavy body and a wide head.

LIFECYCLE

The female lays about twenty eggs and then stays wrapped around them until they hatch and leave.

HABITAT

The diamond python lives in bushland along the coastal areas of New South Wales. It also lives in roof spaces and in sheds near homes and farms.

FOOD

Pythons wait until a rat or mouse comes near and then they pounce on it. Pythons coil their body around their prey, stopping it from breathing and crushing it until they kill it.

CONSERVATION

The main threat to pythons is the clearing of their bushland habitat near towns and cities. A feral cat or dog trying to attack a fully-grown python is likely to become dinner rather than get a meal for itself.

VENOM AND BITING

Pythons do not have venom, but their strong jaws and sharp teeth will cause a very painful wound if one bites you.

FACT

A diamond python will kill and eat a pet dog that has been chained up and cannot get away.

FACT FILE

Length: about 3 metres
Colour: grey and cream diamond pattern
Venomous: no
Habitat: bushland in southeastern Australia
Life span: up to 20 years
Scientific name: *Morelia spilota spilota*

FACT

Diamond pythons often live in roof spaces, where they feed on rats and mice.

MORE AUSTRALIAN SNAKES

BROWN TREE SNAKE

GREEN TREE SNAKE

KEELBACK

CARPET PYTHON

DUGITE

CHILDREN'S PYTHON
WHITE-LIPPED SNAKE
SMALL-EYED SNAKE
BANDY-BANDY

WORLD'S MOST VENOMOUS SNAKES

COASTAL TAIPAN, AUSTRALIA

BANDED KRAIT, INDIA

EASTERN BROWN SNAKE, AUSTRALIA

BOOMSLANG, AFRICA

QUESTION & ANSWER

What's the difference between poisonous and venomous?

A:

- Venomous means having poison that is injected using fangs or stingers
- Poisonous means having poison that is spread by touching, swallowing or spitting

KING COBRA, INDIA

INLAND TAIPAN, AUSTRALIA

BLACK MAMBA, AFRICA

TIGER SNAKE, AUSTRALIA

SNAKE BASIC FACTS

Fossil snakes found in Australia are over thirty million years old

Snakes produce young by laying eggs or by giving birth to live snakes

Snakes have scales

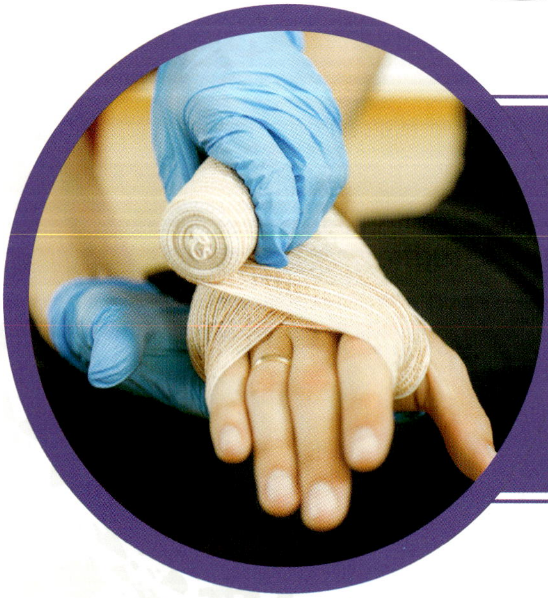

DEATHS FROM SNAKE BITE

Despite having some of the deadliest snakes in the world, Australia is fortunate in only recording about two deaths each year from snake bites. Most of the hundreds of people who end up in hospital each year after an encounter with a snake will fully recover after treatment with antivenom.

SHEDDING

Snakes grow by shedding their outer layer of skin. These dry, shed skins are often the only sign you will find that you have a snake in your shed or roof space.

Snakes are reptiles without legs

Snakes are cold-blooded. They need the warmth from the sun to heat their body and give them enough energy to start moving

Snakes are carnivores and important predators in the natural environment

Snakes twist their body from side to side and send ripples along their length to help push their body along

SNAKE ADAPTATIONS

JAW

A snake's front lower jaw is not joined in the middle. This is how it can stretch its mouth so wide that it can eat an animal that is bigger than its own head.

STAYING ALIVE

Without their sharp teeth, lightning-fast movements and venomous fangs, snakes would be very vulnerable and easily attacked by predators.

VENOM

Snake venom is made in glands in the snake's head. It is injected by being pumped down the hollow tubes in specialised teeth called fangs.

SNAKE MILKED FOR ANTIVENOM

The split tongue is used instead of a nose and can detect scents in the air

CAMOUFLAGE

Snakes in Australia mostly use camouflage both to hide from predators and to hide from prey until they are ready to attack it. Their body colours make them look like stones, pebbles, sand or dead leaves.

HEARING

Snakes don't have external ears but can feel sound as vibrations through their bodies

SNAKES AS PETS

In Australia, all native snakes are protected animals, which means that they cannot be removed from or released into the bush. Killing any native animal is also unlawful.

Laws for keeping snakes as pets vary in each State and Territory. Those that do allow keeping a native snake insist that it is obtained from a licensed dealer. You usually need to apply for your own reptile licence as well. In New South Wales, snakes from other countries cannot be kept as pets.

FACT

The poisonous, feral cane toad has killed countless native snakes.

GLOSSARY

Snake Word List

antivenom	medicine used to treat snake bite
carnivore	eats other animals
dorsal	on the back
fangs	hollow teeth used to inject venom
paralyse	make unable to move
poisonous	having poison that is spread by touch or spitting
potent	strong
toxic	poisonous
venom	poison produced by an animal for injection into prey or a predator
venomous	having poison that is injected using fangs

FEAR OF SNAKES

Most humans seem to have an inbuilt fear of snakes, as do many other animals. Caged birds will instinctively become terrified if they see a snake, even though they have never been exposed to one before. Evolution has made us afraid so that we keep away and stay alive.

INDEX

adaptations 6, 19, 28
antivenom 26, 28, 31
birth 11, 14, 16, 18, 26
eggs 4-6, 8, 11, 12, 14, 16, 18, 20, 26
fangs 5, 7, 8, 16, 17, 25, 28, 31
fear 5, 16, 31
fierce snake 9
gardens 4, 5, 10
snakes as pets 30
tongue 8, 29